TO:

_____

FROM:

_____

DATE:

_____

"Come to me, all of you who are weary
and burdened, and I will give you rest."
~Matthew 11:28~

Don't worry about anything, but in everything,
through prayer and petition with thanksgiving,
present your requests to God.
~Philippians 4:6~

Rejoice always, pray constantly, give thanks in everything;
for this is God's will for you in Christ Jesus.
~1 Thessalonians 5:16-18~

Be strong and courageous; don't be terrified or afraid of them. For the LORD your God is the one who will go with you; he will not leave you or abandon you.
~Deuteronomy 31:6~

*Let us run with endurance the race that lies
before us, keeping our eyes on Jesus,
the source and perfecter of our faith.*
~Hebrews 12:1-2~

Take delight in the LORD, and he will
give you your heart's desires.
~Psalm 37:4~

"Love the Lord your God with all your heart, with all your soul, and with all your mind."
~Matthew 22:37~

And be kind and compassionate to
one another, forgiving one another, just
as God also forgave you in Christ.
~Ephesians 4:32~

*For you are saved by grace through faith,
and this is not from yourselves; it is God's gift—
not from works, so that no one can boast.
~Ephesians 2:8-9~*

I have been crucified with Christ,
and I no longer live, but Christ lives in me.
~Galatians 2:20~

For we are his workmanship, created in
Christ Jesus for good works, which God
prepared ahead of time for us to do.
~Ephesians 2:10~

The one who walks with the wise will become wise,
but a companion of fools will suffer harm.
~Proverbs 13:20~

"Haven't I commanded you: be strong and
courageous? Do not be afraid or discouraged,
for the LORD your God is with you wherever you go."
~Joshua 1:9~

Trust in the LORD forever, because in the LORD,
the LORD himself, is an everlasting rock!
~Isaiah 26:4~

*Do nothing out of selfish ambition
or conceit, but in humility consider others
as more important than yourselves.
~Philippians 2:3~*

_____

Blessed is the one who endures trials, because
when he has stood the test he will receive the crown
of life that God has promised to those who love him.
~James 1:12~

Because of the LORD's faithful love we do not
perish, for his mercies never end. They are new
every morning; great is your faithfulness!
~Lamentations 3:22-23~

Therefore we do not give up. Even though
our outer person is being destroyed, our inner
person is being renewed day by day.
~2 Corinthians 4:16~

Do not be conformed to this age, but be transformed
by the renewing of your mind, so that you may discern
what is the good, pleasing, and perfect will of God.
~Romans 12:2~

_____

Trust in the LORD with all your heart,
and do not rely on your own understanding.
~Proverbs 3:5~

For the word of God is living and effective and sharper
than any double-edged sword, penetrating as far as
the separation of soul and spirit, joints and marrow. It is able
to judge the thoughts and intentions of the heart.
~Hebrews 4:12~

_____

The Lord does not delay his promise, as some
understand delay, but is patient with you, not wanting
any to perish but all to come to repentance.
~2 Peter 3:9~

"The LORD your God is among you, a warrior who saves. He will rejoice over you with gladness. He will be quiet in his love. He will delight in you with singing."
~Zephaniah 3:17~

_____

But I know that my Redeemer lives,
and at the end he will stand on the dust.
~Job 19:25~

"Come to me, all of you who are weary
and burdened, and I will give you rest."
~Matthew 11:28~

_____

Don't worry about anything, but in everything,
through prayer and petition with thanksgiving,
present your requests to God.
~Philippians 4:6~

Rejoice always, pray constantly, give thanks in everything;
for this is God's will for you in Christ Jesus.
~1 Thessalonians 5:16–18~

_____

Be strong and courageous; don't be terrified
or afraid of them. For the LORD your God is the one who
will go with you; he will not leave you or abandon you."
~Deuteronomy 31:6~

Let us run with endurance the race that lies before us, keeping our eyes on Jesus, the source and perfecter of our faith.
~Hebrews 12:1-2~

_Take delight in the LORD, and he will
give you your heart's desires._
~Psalm 37:4~

"Love the Lord your God with all your heart,
with all your soul, and with all your mind."
~Matthew 22:37~

And be kind and compassionate to
one another, forgiving one another, just
as God also forgave you in Christ.
~Ephesians 4:32~

For you are saved by grace through faith,
and this is not from yourselves; it is God's gift—
not from works, so that no one can boast.
~Ephesians 2:8–9~

I have been crucified with Christ,
and I no longer live, but Christ lives in me.
~Galatians 2:20~

For we are his workmanship, created in
Christ Jesus for good works, which God
prepared ahead of time for us to do.
~Ephesians 2:10~

The one who walks with the wise will become wise,
but a companion of fools will suffer harm.
~Proverbs 13:20~

"Haven't I commanded you: be strong and courageous? Do not be afraid or discouraged, for the LORD your God is with you wherever you go."
~Joshua 1:9~

Trust in the LORD forever, because in the LORD,
the LORD himself, is an everlasting rock!
~Isaiah 26:4~

*Do nothing out of selfish ambition
or conceit, but in humility consider others
as more important than yourselves.*
~Philippians 2:3~

Blessed is the one who endures trials, because
when he has stood the test he will receive the crown
of life that God has promised to those who love him.
~James 1:12~

_____

_____
_____
_____
_____
_____
_____
_____
_____
_____
_____
_____
_____
_____
_____
_____
_____
_____
_____

*Because of the LORD's faithful love we do not
perish, for his mercies never end. They are new
every morning; great is your faithfulness!*
~Lamentations 3:22–23~

Therefore we do not give up. Even though our outer person is being destroyed, our inner person is being renewed day by day.
~2 Corinthians 4:16~

Do not be conformed to this age, but be transformed
by the renewing of your mind, so that you may discern
what is the good, pleasing, and perfect will of God.
~Romans 12:2~

_____

Trust in the LORD with all your heart,
and do not rely on your own understanding.
~proverbs 3:5~

For the word of God is living and effective and sharper
than any double-edged sword, penetrating as far as
the separation of soul and spirit, joints and marrow. It is able
to judge the thoughts and intentions of the heart.
~Hebrews 4:12~

The Lord does not delay his promise, as some understand delay, but is patient with you, not wanting any to perish but all to come to repentance.
~2 Peter 3:9~

"The LORD your God is among you, a warrior who saves.
He will rejoice over you with gladness. He will be
quiet in his love. He will delight in you with singing."
~Zephaniah 3:17~

But I know that my Redeemer lives,
and at the end he will stand on the dust.
~Job 19:25~

"Come to me, all of you who are weary
and burdened, and I will give you rest."
~Matthew 11:28~

*Don't worry about anything, but in everything,
through prayer and petition with thanksgiving,
present your requests to God.*
~Philippians 4:6~

Rejoice always, pray constantly, give thanks in everything;
for this is God's will for you in Christ Jesus.
~1 Thessalonians 5:16-18~

_____

Be strong and courageous; don't be terrified
or afraid of them. For the LORD your God is the one who
will go with you; he will not leave you or abandon you."
~Deuteronomy 31:6~

Let us run with endurance the race that lies
before us, keeping our eyes on Jesus,
the source and perfecter of our faith.
~Hebrews 12:1-2~

Take delight in the LORD, and he will
give you your heart's desires.
~Psalm 37:4~

*"Love the Lord your God with all your heart,
with all your soul, and with all your mind."*
~Matthew 22:37~

_And be kind and compassionate to
one another, forgiving one another, just
as Go also forgave you in Christ._
~Ephesians 4:32~

For you are saved by grace through faith,
and this is not from yourselves; it is God's gift—
not from works, so that no one can boast.
~Ephesians 2:8-9~

I have been crucified with Christ,
and I no longer live, but Christ lives in me.
~Galatians 2:20~

For we are his workmanship, created in
Christ Jesus for good works, which God
prepared ahead of time for us to do.
~Ephesians 2:10~

The one who walks with the wise will become wise,
but a companion of fools will suffer harm.
~Proverbs 13:20~

"Haven't I commanded you: be strong and courageous? Do not be afraid or discouraged, for the LORD your God is with you wherever you go."
~Joshua 1:9~

Trust in the LORD forever, because in the LORD,
the LORD himself, is an everlasting rock!
~Isaiah 26:4~

Do nothing out of selfish ambition
or conceit, but in humility consider others
as more important than yourselves.
~Philippians 2:3~

Blessed is the one who endures trials, because
when he has stood the test he will receive the crown
of life that God has promised to those who love him.
~James 1:12~

Because of the LORD's faithful love we do not perish, for his mercies never end. They are new every morning; great is your faithfulness!
~Lamentations 3:22-23~

Therefore we do not give up. Even though
our outer person is being destroyed, our inner
person is being renewed day by day.
~2 Corinthians 4:16~

*Do not be conformed to this age, but be transformed
by the renewing of your mind, so that you may discern
what is the good, pleasing, and perfect will of God.*
~Romans 12:2~

Trust in the LORD with all your heart,
and do not rely on your own understanding.
~Proverbs 3:5~

For the word of God is living and effective and sharper
than any double-edged sword, penetrating as far as
the separation of soul and spirit, joints and marrow. It is able
to judge the thoughts and intentions of the heart.
~Hebrews 4:12~

_____

The Lord does not delay his promise, as some
understand delay, but is patient with you, not wanting
any to perish but all to come to repentance.
~2 Peter 3:9~

"The LORD your God is among you, a warrior who saves.
He will rejoice over you with gladness. He will be
quiet in his love. He will delight in you with singing."
~Zephaniah 3:17~

But I know that my Redeemer lives,
and at the end he will stand on the dust.
~Job 19:25~

"Come to me, all of you who are weary
and burdened, and I will give you rest."
~Matthew 11:28~

Don't worry about anything, but in everything,
through prayer and petition with thanksgiving,
present your requests to God.
~Philippians 4:6~

Rejoice always, pray constantly, give thanks in everything;
for this is God's will for you in Christ Jesus.
~1 Thessalonians 5:16–18~

Be strong and courageous; don't be terrified
or afraid of them. For the LORD your God is the one who
will go with you; he will not leave you or abandon you."
~Deuteronomy 31:6~

Let us run with endurance the race that lies
before us, keeping our eyes on Jesus,
the source and perfecter of our faith.
~Hebrews 12:1-2~

Take delight in the LORD, and he will
give you your heart's desires.
~Psalm 37:4~

_"Love the Lord your God with all your heart,
with all your soul, and with all your mind."_
~Matthew 22:37~

And be kind and compassionate to
one another, forgiving one another, just
as God also forgave you in Christ.
~Ephesians 4:32~

For you are saved by grace through faith,
and this is not from yourselves; it is God's gift—
not from works, so that no one can boast.
~Ephesians 2:8–9~

I have been crucified with Christ,
and I no longer live, but Christ lives in me.
~Galatians 2:20~

For we are his workmanship, created in
Christ Jesus for good works, which God
prepared ahead of time for us to do.
~Ephesians 2:10~

_____

The one who walks with the wise will become wise,
but a companion of fools will suffer harm.
~proverbs 13:20~

"Haven't I commanded you: be strong and courageous? Do not be afraid or discouraged, for the LORD your God is with you wherever you go."
~Joshua 1:9~

Trust in the LORD forever, because in the LORD,
the LORD himself, is an everlasting rock!
~Isaiah 26:4~

Do nothing out of selfish ambition
or conceit, but in humility consider others
as more important than yourselves.
~Philippians 2:3~

_____

Blessed is the one who endures trials, because
when he has stood the test he will receive the crown
of life that God has promised to those who love him.
~James 1:12~

Because of the LORD's faithful love we do not
perish, for his mercies never end. They are new
every morning; great is your faithfulness!
~Lamentations 3:22-23~

Therefore we do not give up. Even though
our outer person is being destroyed, our inner
person is being renewed day by day.
~2 Corinthians 4:16~

Do not be conformed to this age, but be transformed
by the renewing of your mind, so that you may discern
what is the good, pleasing, and perfect will of God.
~Romans 12:2~

Trust in the LORD with all your heart,
and do not rely on your own understanding.
~proverbs 3:5~

For the word of God is living and effective and sharper
than any double-edged sword, penetrating as far as
the separation of soul and spirit, joints and marrow. It is able
to judge the thoughts and intentions of the heart.
~Hebrews 4:12~

The Lord does not delay his promise, as some
understand delay, but is patient with you, not wanting
any to perish but all to come to repentance.
~2 Peter 3:9~

"The LORD your God is among you, a warrior who saves.
He will rejoice over you with gladness. He will be quiet
in his love. He will delight in you with singing."
~Zephaniah 3:17~

But I know that my Redeemer lives,
and at the end he will stand on the dust.
~Job 19:25~

"Come to me, all of you who are weary
and burdened, and I will give you rest."
~Matthew 11:28~

_____

Don't worry about anything, but in everything,
through prayer and petition with thanksgiving,
present your requests to God.
~Philippians 4:6~

Rejoice always, pray constantly, give thanks in everything;
for this is God's will for you in Christ Jesus.
~1 Thessalonians 5:16-18~

Be strong and courageous; don't be terrified
or afraid of them. For the LORD your God is the one who
will go with you; he will not leave you or abandon you.
~Deuteronomy 31:6~

Let us run with endurance the race that lies
before us, keeping our eyes on Jesus,
the source and perfecter of our faith.
~Hebrews 12:1-2~

Take delight in the LORD, and he will
give you your heart's desires.
~Psalm 37:4~

"Love the Lord your God with all your heart,
with all your soul, and with all your mind."
~Matthew 22:37~

_____

And be kind and compassionate to
one another, forgiving one another, just
as God also forgave you in Christ.
~Ephesians 4:32~

*For you are saved by grace through faith,
and this is not from yourselves; it is God's gift—
not from works, so that no one can boast.*
~Ephesians 2:8-9~

I have been crucified with Christ,
and I no longer live, but Christ lives in me.
~Galatians 2:20~

For we are his workmanship, created in
Christ Jesus for good works, which God
prepared ahead of time for us to do.
~Ephesians 2:10~

The one who walks with the wise will become wise,
but a companion of fools will suffer harm.
~proverbs 13:20~

"Haven't I commanded you: be strong and courageous? Do not be afraid or discouraged, for the LORD your God is with you wherever you go."
~Joshua 1:9~

Trust in the LORD forever, because in the LORD,
the LORD himself, is an everlasting rock!.
~Isaiah 26:4~

*Do nothing out of selfish ambition
or conceit, but in humility consider others
as more important than yourselves.*
~Philippians 2:3~

Blessed is the one who endures trials, because
when he has stood the test he will receive the crown
of life that God has promised to those who love him.
~James 1:12~

Because of the LORD's faithful love we do not perish, for his mercies never end. They are new every morning; great is your faithfulness!
~Lamentations 3:22-23~

Therefore we do not give up. Even though
our outer person is being destroyed, our inner
person is being renewed day by day.
~2 Corinthians 4:16~

Do not be conformed to this age, but be transformed
by the renewing of your mind, so that you may discern
what is the good, pleasing, and perfect will of God.
~Romans 12:2~

Trust in the LORD with all your heart,
and do not rely on your own understanding.
~proverbs 3:5~

For the word of God is living and effective and sharper
than any double-edged sword, penetrating as far as
the separation and soul and spirit, joints and marrow. It is able
to judge the thoughts and intentions of the heart.
~Hebrews 4:12~

_____

The Lord does not delay his promise, as some
understand delay, but is patient with you, not wanting
any to perish but all to come to repentance.
~2 Peter 3:9~

"The LORD your God is among you, a warrior who saves.
He will rejoice over you with gladness. He will be
quiet in his love. He will delight in you with singing."
~Zephaniah 3:17~

But I know that my Redeemer lives,
and at the end he will stand on the dust.
~Job 19:25~

"Come to me, all of you who are weary
and burdened, and I will give you rest."
~Matthew 11:28~

Don't worry about anything, but in everything, through prayer and petition with thanksgiving, present your requests to God.
~Philippians 4:6~

Rejoice always, pray constantly, give thanks in everything;
for this is God's will for you in Christ Jesus.
~1 Thessalonians 5:16–18~

Be strong and courageous; don't be terrified
or afraid of them. For the LORD your God is the one who
will go with you; he will not leave you or abandon you."
~Deuteronomy 31:6~

Let us run with endurance the race that lies
before us, keeping our eyes on Jesus,
the source and perfecter of our faith.
~Hebrews 12:1-2~

Take delight in the LORD, and he will
give you your heart's desires.
~Psalm 37:4~